IMAGES
of America

WALWORTH
COUNTY

D1563171

IMAGES
of America

WALWORTH
COUNTY

Walter S. Dunn Jr.

ARCADIA

Published by Arcadia Publishing,
an imprint of Tempus Publishing, Inc.
2 Cumberland Street
Charleston, SC 29401

Printed in Great Britain.

Library of Congress Catalog Card Number: 98-87780

For all general information contact Arcadia Publishing at:
Telephone 843-853-2070
Fax 843-853-0044
E-Mail arcadia@charleston.net

For customer service and orders:
Toll-Free 1-888-313-BOOK

Visit us on the internet at http://www.arcadiaimages.com

CONTENTS

ACKNOWLEDGMENTS

Jean Dunn has made the major contribution to this work, locating the photographs, drafting the captions, and editing the final text. Doris Reinke searched the files of the Walworth County Historical Society for many of the pictures. Photographs also came from the Barth family, the Moyse family, Charlotte Gates, Edward Chesko, John Notz, Evelyn Mehltretter, and the Belfry Theater.

INTRODUCTION

The history of Walworth County is a case study for the technological revolution that dramatically changed the way we live from 1880 to 1950, reflecting the spreading influence of Chicago on the surrounding countryside. The most apparent change was in transportation. By 1880, steam railroads crisscrossed America and provided a network that placed every town within 20 miles of a railroad station.

By 1900, automobiles had been developed that could venture safely into the countryside, although breakdowns were still frequent enough that "get a horse" was a common expression shouted at stranded motorists. The paved roads created for the bicycles of the 1890s provided convenient access to a large hinterland, but beyond those roads, automobiles lacked the power to navigate deep ruts and mud. The horse-drawn wagon therefore had a role as late as the 1930s, when gravel roads replaced most of the muddy roads of the past.

By 1939, the first superhighway had been built in Pennsylvania and the system rapidly expanded with the Highway Act of 1955, improving the convenience of auto travel in competition with the railroads.

Communication techniques changed rapidly, beginning with the telegraph and telephone in the mid-19th century, which became commonplace by 1880. In the early years of the 20th century, radio emerged as our fathers and grandfathers built crystal sets from instructions in magazines. These sets could receive static-filled messages from Chicago and even permit the joy of hearing the voice of Caruso. By 1950, televisions in our homes received programs from around the nation and caused havoc in the movie industry, just as the movies had destroyed vaudeville in the early 20th century.

Economic change was most noticeable in rural counties like Walworth. In

1880, the milk train picked up cans of milk brought to town by horse-drawn wagons. The pickup truck extended the distance from town that a dairy farmer could work, and the bulk milk container trucks eliminated distance as a factor altogether. The small dairy farm began to disappear as larger herds and farms, with expensive, advanced equipment, became more efficient and therefore more profitable. New fertilizers increased the production of each acre, and the small farmer found more profit in producing corn and soybeans, rather than trying to compete with large dairy farms.

With the advent of increasingly improved machinery, a farmer could either acquire more land, to produce larger crops to pay for the machinery, or he could become a part-time farmer. By 1950, industrial parks sprung up around Walworth County as small entrepreneurs built light industry and assembly factories, taking advantage of the non-union, low-wage labor available in small towns. Part-time farmers, their wives, and former hired hands were all eager for the jobs that permitted them to retain all the advantages of safe and healthy small-town life, in contrast to the misery of the city workers.

Along with the rest of the nation, Walworth County witnessed a revolution in education from 1880 to 1950. The many one-room schools, located within walking distance of about 20 or 30 farms, provided up to eight years of basic skills. They were gradually replaced by consolidated schools in the late 1950s, whose students were driven by their parents and, in later years, boarded school busses at their homes. With the rapid expansion of communication and transportation, farm families no longer removed their boys from school as soon as they could work, but allowed them to remain in school to gain the knowledge needed to compete in the outside world.

To a greater extent than most rural counties, recreation played a vital role in the changes that occurred in Walworth County. Even before the railroad reached the county, the quality of life on beautiful Geneva Lake attracted Chicago's up-scale residents. In contrast to the miserable heat of even the finest homes in Chicago during the summer, a home on the south shore of Lake Geneva offered pleasant days of sailing and swimming and cool nights for rest. When the railroads reached the Geneva Lake area, families from Chicago came for the summer. The private steam launches that greeted the trains in the 1890s were replaced with luxurious power boats by the 1930s. The weekends were marked with elegant parties and arrival in your own power boat.

By 1950, a further change took place as the declining price of power boats and the construction of highways made possible the arrival of more and more residents from the Chicago area, ready to absorb the pleasures of Geneva Lake. The city of Lake Geneva became a Mecca for weekend visitors, many towing their power boats on trailers and buying summer homes on the evermore-crowded available land near the lake.

One

IN THE BEGINNING
THERE WAS FARMING

From the very beginnings of Walworth County, the leading industry was subsistence farming, which meant growing food for the family. Later, with the development of fertilizers and hybrid seeds, farmers could sell some of their crops. The enormous expanse of flat tillable land on the northern part of the Big Foot Prairie made it easier to prepare the fields. In the mid-19th century, the cradle was a vast improvement over the scythe. The cradle kept the grain stalks together and the second man could rake sheaves more easily.

Having only a few horses (usually one team and a spare), the small farmer of the mid-19th century had difficulty plowing the hills that tired the horses. Most of the early settlement was therefore on the choice Big Foot Prairie in the southern half of the county.

Manpower and horsepower worked the farms until the mid-20th century. Grain shocks were tossed by hand onto a wagon, which was then pulled to the threshing machine.

Stubble was piled high with a makeshift set of forks and pulleys. Even the women helped do this tedious work.

Cultivating corn was a long process during the heat of the summer. Children brought jars of cool water from the milk house for their thirsty, hard-working fathers.

"Prince" has time for a rest in 1912.

Horse-drawn wagons brought corn bundles to fill the silo for winter feed in September 1927.

A team readies for work during the winter of 1912.

13

Farm wives worked hard, caring for chickens, calves, gardens, and children, in addition to regular household chores.

The thresher, which separated the grain from the straw, was a standby for many years before the combine speeded up the harvesting and made it possible for farmers to work larger farms.

Feeding the cattle during the winter was basic to dairying, and silage was the answer. Here, a new silo was under construction, with the aid of pulleys and horsepower to pull up the cement blocks.

The critical need to harvest at the proper time and the enormous demand for labor led to harvesting crews of neighbors moving from farm to farm in the fall. Horses were needed to reap the grain and haul it to the threshing machine powered by a steam engine. Whoever had his grain harvested last one year would be first the next.

Custom operators traveled around the community to do threshing and shredding. The operator fired up the engine early in the morning to have steam by starting time.

Raking up the stubble was a backbreaking task.

Straw was blown into a stack, to use as bedding for the cattle and horses.

With steam power, the grain was quickly separated from the chaff and ready for market. The long leather belt was necessary to prevent sparks from the steam engine igniting the straw.

Steam engines were used for many purposes around the farm. Here, steam power is used to saw logs for firewood.

Another community project was barn raising. In 1912, the frames of this barn had been assembled on the ground and were then hoisted to a vertical position by many hands. When completed, the barn was initiated with a barn dance for all the neighborhood.

The first step was to cut all the pieces needed for the barn frame and drill holes.

The tractor brought machine power to the field and sped up the transformation from wheat to corn as the major crop. The tractors pulled the ploughs and disks in the spring to prepare the soil for planting.

This Case tractor sped up the work immensely.

A working dairy farm needed a windmill to pump water to cool the milk and to water the stock. Later, the windmill was first replaced by a gasoline engine, and then by electric motors.

The tractor was the essential power source for many implements. It came along at a time when hired help became scarce, as young men moved to the cities for factory jobs, rather than remaining in the country as hired hands. Horses required endless hours of care and grooming, while the tractor needed only fuel and occasional repair.

A team of horses surveys its replacement in 1939. In the fall, the tractor pulled the corn binder, which made the bundles to be shocked and hauled to the shredder.

The farmer drives the tractor while his wife watches the operation of the corn binder.

Some farmers powered their own shredding machines with tractors.

Both the farmers and the horses were relieved with the arrival of the combine in the early 1940s, which simplified harvesting.

In the spring, nearly every farmer had a colt to break. Usually, the colt wore both a halter and a bridle, with the halter tied to the side of the dependable horse.

In the fall, the lengthening shadows marked the end of the growing season and the hard labor of planting, cultivating, and harvesting the crop.

To prepare for Thanksgiving dinner, the farmer raised a turkey and planted squash and pumpkins.

Little boys fed the calves with a bottle when the mother cow's milk was not yet available.

The quiet, black-faced sheep, a source of wool and mutton, enjoyed posing with the farm boy.

Dairying was Walworth County's main industry for many decades. Large barns housed from 20 to 50 cows. A hired hand or older son was needed to complete all the tasks of the farmer.

The availability of lush meadows in the ideal climate of southern Wisconsin was the key to successful dairying.

To supplement grazing, the farmer raised field crops to feed his cows. Cash crops were secondary.

The farms on the Big Foot Prairie produced bountiful crops of corn that were "almost as high as an elephant's eye."

The farmers of Walworth County descended for the most part from the early German settlers who came to Wisconsin in the mid-19th century to escape the turmoil that followed the Revolution of 1848. Liberal governments in the various small provinces of Germany were overturned by authoritarian rulers, depriving the people of freedom and imposing heavy taxes on them. Many came to Wisconsin in search of freedom and economic opportunity, and to escape compulsory military service in Germany. The immigrants brought with them the desire to work hard and succeed.

This second-generation German farmer still retained the values of his father, who had come from a farm near Berlin with the determination to succeed.

Little girls line the steps of this farmhouse in 1934. Wash tubs hanging on the wall await their big day on Monday and the Saturday night bath ritual.

This family, photographed in 1930, had no matching washer and dryer.

Little girls on the farm did not have many toys, but had live animals to play with. A future farm wife makes the acquaintance of a hungry-looking piglet.

If a boy had a straw hat and a hoe, he could pretend he was a farmer like his father. The door (left) provided easy access to the cellar. Cyclone cellars were used to store produce, and also served as shelter during threatening weather.

Life on the farm was harsh during the winter, and families were often cut off from the town for days by snow-clogged roads.

Despite the weather, the animals had to be cared for. The cattle had to be fed and the horses groomed.

Two

THE FARMERS
CREATED SMALL TOWNS

The Walworth County Court House in Elkhorn, sketched in 1873, was the center of government and legal affairs. In the early 19th century, the major factors that created a town in rural areas were government and law. After 1870, the essential factor for a prosperous small town in Walworth County was a railroad depot, where the farmers could deliver their milk each morning to be loaded on the "milk train" for Chicago. Towns had to be close together to eliminate the need for a long trip each day.

The daily trip meant that practically every family within a 10-mile radius would send one person to town each day. This provided a considerable customer base for the merchants, because once the milk was delivered, the farmer went shopping for food, clothing, and services. On Saturday, the entire family went to town in a horse-drawn wagon for shopping and socializing.

Built in 1836, the Webster House (now a museum) was originally located on the square in Elkhorn as the land office. In 1857, the house was moved to Rockwell Street and became the home of Joseph Philbrick Webster (1819–1875), a composer of hymns and patriotic songs in the 1860s.

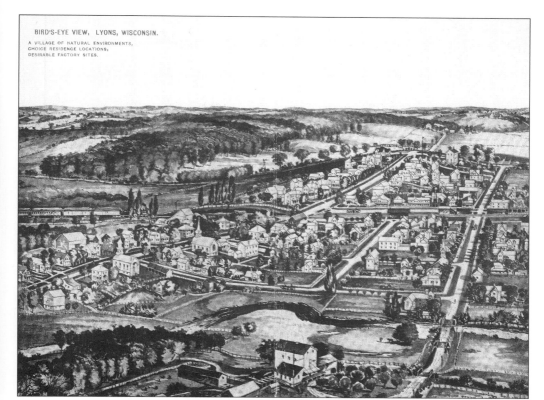

BIRD'S-EYE VIEW, LYONS, WISCONSIN.

A VILLAGE OF NATURAL ENVIRONMENTS,
CHOICE RESIDENCE LOCATIONS,
DESIRABLE FACTORY SITES.

The village of Lyons, pictured in 1909, reflected the importance of the railroad (upper left corner). Activity centered on the depot (upper right corner), which was flanked by a few stores.

WALWORTH AVE., DELAVAN, WIS.

The automobile changed the appearance of town life, but not the tempo. In the 1920s, cars replaced horses and carriages in Delavan, and cobblestones paved the main street. The family could drive to larger towns like Delavan for shopping, ending the monopoly of small towns.

37

Plain Street, Sharon, WI   circa 1900

Around 1900, Sharon, another town on the railroad, had a livery stable on Plain Street for boarding or hiring horses. Note the gas street light and the telephone pole to the right with many crossbars.

The shopping center located near the railroad depot served the needs of the farmers around 1905.

A well-groomed horse reflected the farmer's pride for one of his most valued possessions, even in 1939.

The farmhouse of 1900 was a simple frame building with no pretense of landscaping.

In 1950, stately elms lined the square in Walworth Village, still the center of activity and located south of the railroad depot. U.S. Highway 14, the gateway to Wisconsin, passed alongside the square, which became an avenue of heavy traffic before the interstate highways were built.

The electric trolley tracks ran north on Main Street in Walworth Village, bringing passengers from Harvard to Fontana on Geneva Lake. The street was lined with retail stores for the farmers visiting the town.

Large homes, such as this Maple Avenue residence, were owned by the merchants and businessmen in Walworth Village.

Although few visitors stayed overnight, the Wayside Hotel on the north side of the village square was the successor to the Red Lion Hotel, built in 1842.

The rural Baptist Brick Church, northwest of Walworth Village, was built in 1844. Later, through the efforts of its pastor and congregation, the saloon in Walworth was forced out of business. Religion was an important part of small-town life.

Cyrus Church, born in 1817, was one of the area's earliest settlers. Church came to Wisconsin in 1837 and established a successful farm near Walworth. Very active in community affairs, he later built this elegant residence on his farm. His descendants still live in Walworth Village.

Three
RECREATION—
THE SECOND INDUSTRY

A couple peacefully enjoys Lake Delavan in 1913 in Sunday attire. The beauty of Lake Geneva and other lakes in Walworth County attracted the attention of the prominent Chicagoans in the second half of the 19th century. The completion of the railroads from Chicago to the northwest that passed through Walworth County provided easy access to the area. The combination of comparatively cool summers (before air conditioning), close proximity to the city, comfortable rail connections, and beautiful lakes made Walworth County a Mecca for the wealthy families of Chicago.

During the 1940s, the emergence of a more affluent middle class brought thousands more from Illinois to the lakes of Walworth County, at first renting and then bringing their own boats in tow. A landing at the YMCA camp in Williams Bay featured a flotilla of canoes for the entertainment of the campers.

Later, a small summer home used only on the weekend was affordable, and air conditioning had made Chicago bearable the rest of the week. With "lake privileges," the summer homes were a base for weekend fun with a motor boat, for fishing, swimming, and, later, water skiing. Inboard motor boats became the prestigious craft of the 1940s, replacing the small steam launches.

The automobile made day trips to the lake possible. Bathing suits were still "modesty personified."

Driving to the beach at Fontana on Lake Geneva was a common pastime for young couples—dashing young men in straw hats, like "Slim" Cunningham, and ladies in their Sunday best. Although the lady pictured here is behind the wheel, usually men drove.

Modesty was still the order of the day in the 1920s for bathing beauties on Lake Geneva.

Little children could sit on the sand with tiny waves lapping at their feet before the giant resorts brought water skiers chasing roaring boats and new vacationers to the lakes to compete with the old-money elite who peacefully enjoyed the water in their stately steam boats. This lady's rubber boots protected her feet from the pebbles in the crystal-clear water of Lake Geneva.

There was nothing better than an automobile inner tube for floating on the lake.

By 1920, swimming suits became more practical and swimming more acceptable, rather than simply wading in elaborate costumes.

The 1930s and 1940s saw a mass invasion of the Lake Geneva beach near the Riviera, which opened in 1933 as a marina and dance hall. "Big bands" from all over America entertained at the Riviera.

The boat landing was in front of Whiting House, opened in 1873, an elegant hotel which once graced the shore of Lake Geneva.

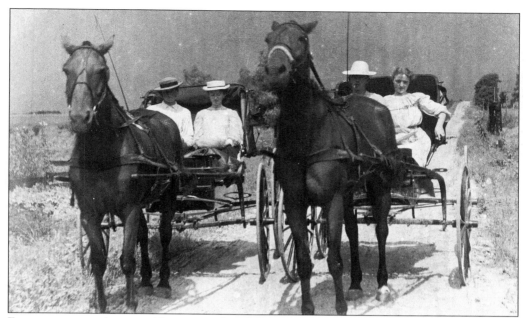

For young men, a horse and buggy was the ultimate status symbol, and it was difficult to attract a girlfriend without one. The lightweight, two-passenger carriages were designed for speed rather than comfort. Moving at a fast trot over the rough gravel roads was a bumpy ride.

Recreation in Walworth County also meant "wheels," and if you could not afford a car then a homemade replica could be pushed around. The push cars, with at least one to push and one to ride, provided hours of fun for these farm boys in 1913.

A tricycle was a highly prized gift for any little girl, but there were no sidewalks in the country for maximum enjoyment.

For a young boy, a bicycle with balloon tires took him to visit his friends who lived miles away. A carrier mounted over the rear wheel was an awkward seat for the passenger. Even though pedaling with bare feet made calluses, shoes were seldom worn during the summer.

Innovative minds made a wagon wheel merry-go-round.

The real joy was the ride, even in a homemade wagon built in 1930, long enough for at least a half dozen tiny tots. The 55-gallon gasoline drums indicate that this farm had already acquired machine power.

A favorite form of year-round recreation was riding horses. Bill Wendeberg, of rural Walworth, rides his sister's pony, Bobby, on a summer day in 1939.

In the winter, sleigh riding was an exciting family pastime in Walworth County, with horses trotting to the jingle of sleigh bells. Almost every family had a sleigh, not only for fun, but also for trips over the snow to town for supplies.

Children and even adults on the farm made up games for entertainment, or played old favorites like "follow the leader," "pom pull-away," "tag," or "hide and seek."

Climbing was always a challenge and an opportunity to show off, even in Sunday-best clothes, as seen in this c. 1912 image.

Playing in the fields and blowing in the wind was always fun.

Climbing the straw stack on a ladder was an adventurous way to catch every little summer breeze.

Normally just hanging around in bib overalls filled most long, summer days.

Taking a good aim in the woods saved ammunition for the man who took hunting seriously.

Happy was the man who could take his wife fishing!

Hunting was not so much a sport for Paul Barth and his grandson, George Wendeberg, as a necessity to add to the family food supply.

Entertainment included listening to speeches. There was always time for commemorating the past. Dr. Paul Jenkins dedicated a historical marker in Fontana in 1927.

The Belfry Theater, north of Williams Bay, started in 1888 as a Mormon meetinghouse. Later, the Belfry became a summer stock theater, where fine actors gained experience, including Paul Newman and Gary Berghoff of Delavan, who became famous as "Radar" in the TV show *Mash*. Later, the theater became the home of the *Eddie Cash Musical Show*.

Even horses watched horses at the racetrack at the Walworth County Fair in 1909. The five-day fair continues to be a major event in Walworth County.

The Young Men's Christian Association, always a mainstay of hospitality and recreation for boys, included track and field competition at the camp in Lake Geneva.

The Elkhorn Cornet Band, shown here in 1911, played for many occasions.

Everybody loved a parade. Fred Platts, riding his dancing horse, Lady, led the 1948 Memorial Day Parade in Elkhorn.

In 1915, the Memorial Day parade in Elkhorn, on an unpaved street, was in sharp contrast to the parade 33 years later. The pump and windmill sign reminds us that before electricity came to the countryside, wind was used to pump water from the wells.

Patriotism was a major influence on small-town life. Here, in 1916, the women of the National Service School trained on the shore of Lake Geneva, long before women became part of the armed services.

A boy and his dog have always been devoted companions exploring the great outdoors.

Most farms had only a single dog, but the arrival of a new litter meant hours of fun.

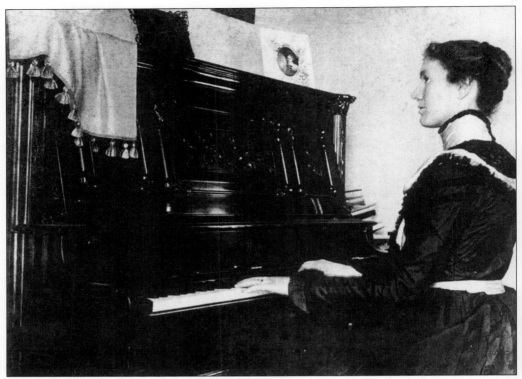

The piano was common entertainment for many families in the 19th century.

The advent of television in the 1950s changed life on the farm and brought the boys inside for entertainment.

Four

THE LAKE PEOPLE—
THE ESCAPE FROM CHICAGO

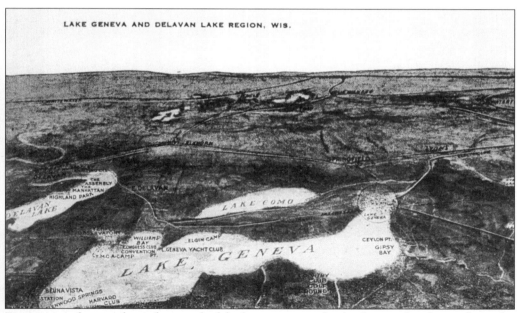

LAKE GENEVA AND DELAVAN LAKE REGION, WIS.

Enterprising farmers from the east had little interest in the land immediately touching the shores of Lake Geneva. However, the land was appealing as a retreat to the mighty industrialists who were developing Chicago as a marketplace for the agrarian economy, through financial and trade institutions. To escape the hot Chicago summers, wealthy families would move to their summer home on Lake Geneva as soon as the school vacation began.

"Black Point," the summer residence built in 1877 by Conrad Seipp (1825–1890), graces the summit of the Black Point peninsula. The name alludes to the abundance of Black Oak trees. Conrad Seipp came to the U.S. from Germany in 1849 and made his fortune in brewing in Chicago. The mansion, originally called "Die Loreley," a German mythical character, was changed to "Black Point" during World War I, when many German names were changed.

"Maple Lawn," the residence of Shelton Sturges, completed in 1873, was the first summer estate on Lake Geneva, and his yacht *Arrow*, built in 1874, was the first private steamer. The excursion steamer pictured right is the first *Lady of the Lake*, launched in 1873. The Lake Geneva Seminary, a boarding school for girls built in 1870, appears in the upper left.

HOME OF J. H. MOORE, LAKE GENEVA, WIS.

An entire social environment was created that duplicated the high society of Chicago. Fashionable parties on the weekend, competition to build a fine house, sailing regattas, and tennis tournaments brought the families together into a closely-knit society. "Loramoor" was the residence of James H. Moore (1852–1916), horse lover supreme. His "Talley Ho" carriage drove the township roads every afternoon. Two of his enterprises were the Diamond Match Company and the National Biscuit Company.

Residence of J. J. Mitchell, Lake Geneva, Wis.

"Ceylon Court" was the residence of John J. Mitchell, the dean of Chicago Banking. Mitchell purchased the building, a reproduction of a Buddhist temple, at the 1893 Colombian Exposition in Chicago. The disassembled building was shipped in 26 boxcars to the shore of Lake Geneva.

The Chicago & Northwestern line between Chicago and Williams Bay served as a commuter train for the lake residents, who then crossed Lake Geneva in steamers to their grand estates dotting the shore.

A graceful steamer glides past Ceylon Court at Manning's Point.

The Lake Geneva Country Club clubhouse, the center of social life for the south shore residents, was constructed in 1916 and designed by Robert B. Spencer Jr. Spencer was influenced by Frank Lloyd Wright's Prairie School of design.

Lake Geneva, Wis. William's Bay Landing.

The Williams Bay landing in the early 1900s exemplifies the approaching automobile age, with horse carriages and lake steamers intermingled.

With the advent of better roads and automobiles, passenger service declined on the railroads. Summer residents came by car, reaching their homes on private drives branching off lakeshore roads. Later arrivals visited or established homes on other lakes in Walworth County. The Sterlingworth Hotel was a famous landmark on Lauderdale Lakes.

Brunnum's Cottage, on Lauderdale Lakes, had a nearby boat shed. Lake frontage was essential for boating.

The "Mortons," on Lauderdale Lakes, was an example of the large comfortable homes built as summer residences.

Middle Lake was a popular vacation spot on Lauderdale Lakes.

The Andy Gump statue in Flat Iron Park, Lake Geneva, originated about 1917. Sydney Smith, the creator of the cartoon character in the *Chicago Tribune*, had a summer home on the lake. Constant vandalism of the statue for over half a century expressed the antagonism between the lake people and the locals. There was little contact with the locals other than hiring servants to assist their Chicago servants, who maintained the estates.

Five

BUSINESS FOR LOCALS AND LAKE PEOPLE

All farming economies share fundamental limiting factors that shape the environment. In the 19th century, every farm needed a "cash crop," something that could be sold in the nearest town for cash to be used to purchase sugar, flour, coffee, salt, clothing, shoes, tools, and other items not produced on the farm. In Walworth County, the first cash crop was wheat. During the Civil War, Wisconsin was one of the leading producers of wheat. Farmers took their bags of wheat to Geneva Flour Mills in horse-drawn wagons and lingered to learn the latest news.

To serve the increasing flow of cash, resulting from the switch to dairying and the arrival of the summer residents, the merchants and other businesses in the small towns prospered. The Elkhorn Lumber Company sold building materials that were delivered to them by rail. Customers loaded the lumber on horse-drawn wagons for delivery.

While in town, farmers would stop at the various stores for supplies. Here in Delavan, the stores were crowded side by side, like a mall. Included were F.C. Dinsmore's hardware and grocery store, which also sold shoes, and a drugstore. Deliveries were made by a horse-drawn wagon, which served to advertise as well.

Horses frequently needed new shoes, which wore out or became loose from constant wear. In 1915, the blacksmith had a large supply of various sizes, ready to re-shoe a horse on demand.

In the smaller towns, like Peck's Station, located north of Elkhorn, friendly faces dispensed groceries and dry goods to customers who came in horse-drawn buggies. Peck Station was on the Eagle Branch, laid in 1870, of the Western Union Railroad.

Light industry had an early start in Wisconsin. Here, workers are assembling band instruments at the Holton Factory in Elkhorn, which is still in business. Notice the high proportion of women employees.

While retailing would continue to be a major business in Walworth County, the cheese factory became an important part of the dairy industry. Farmers who did not sell Grade A milk for shipment to Chicago sent their milk to local cheese factories for the manufacture of Wisconsin's most famous product.

Six

GOOD ROADS AFFECT WALWORTH COUNTY

Roads and automobiles were like the chicken and the egg—without good roads, the early automobiles and trucks with small motors and fragile transmissions broke down so often that "get a horse" became a common expression. The large wheels of the horse-drawn wagons and carriages could overcome most ruts, but not this Millard truck in 1922, near Abells Corner on Highways 12 and 67.

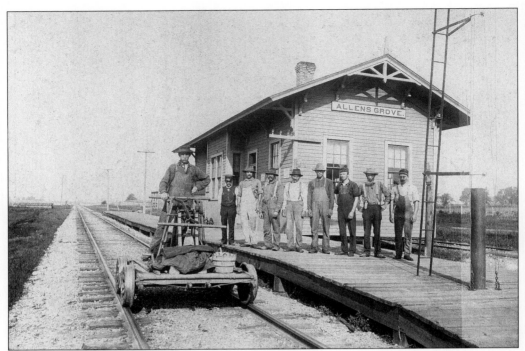

The railroads were essential before good roads were built, but even the rails needed constant maintenance. This crew at Allen's Grove in 1902 used a hand car to carry them down the rails to replace rotten ties and ballast. Before the automobile, gravel roads were adequate in the country because of little traffic.

The development of good gravel roads and blacktop and concrete highways was essential for the dairy farmer. The roads followed previous paths such as this one, alongside a stream that powered a water mill in Delavan in 1907.

The dirt roads at least tied the farms to the towns. On this farm, the windmill pumped cold water from the well to the milk house to keep the milk cool until it was carried to town the next morning.

Every day, some dairy farmers took their milk to creameries such as the Grove Creamery at Bower's Corners, and brought home whey, the waste product, to feed to pigs.

The mailman was perhaps the farm's most welcome visitor. On a hot summer day, frequent stops to rest the horse under the shade of a tree were a necessity.

Our Mail at the Old Mill, Lauderdale Lakes, near Elkhorn, Wis.

Here the mailbox was scarcely needed, as a group of eager pioneers met the mailman, possibly to receive their new Sears, Roebuck catalog.

During the rainy season, especially every spring, dirt roads and poorer gravel roads would become bottomless pits of mud. After a few vehicles had passed, the ruts became deeper and deeper.

Rains flooded both the roads and the fields during spring and fall, the seasons when dairy farmers needed the roads most and could not wait for the sun to dry out the mess.

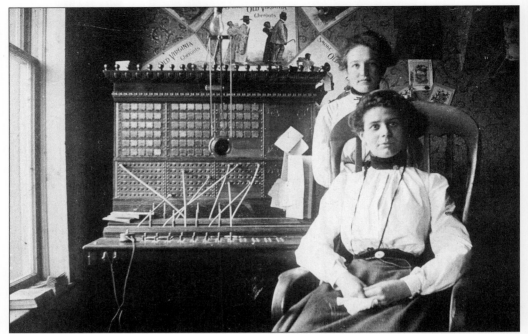

"Number please" was the c. 1900 greeting of telephone operators, plugging wires into switchboards that brought instant news to the farm. Farm life became more exciting with shared party lines, when one could listen to others, and when trips became routine on the improved roads, not only to town but to major cities.

In 1949, Evelyn Hollenbeck Mehltretter of Fontana was a telephone operator in the Lake Geneva office of the Wisconsin Bell Telephone Company.

Seven
THE AUTOMOBILE ARRIVES

The horse had been the most dependable source of motive power on the farm and in the towns for centuries, both for work and recreation. Pictured here, in 1913, Bonnie pulled a two-seat buggy, called a "Piano Box" because of its similarity to the cases used to ship pianos. Note the netting over the horse to protect her from flies.

Everybody went to town on Saturday, making the most of the trip and giving the horse a full load.

In 1914, J.V. Seymour of Lake Geneva delivered ice in 25-pound blocks for home iceboxes, before electric refrigerators were a standard household appliance. Horse-drawn wagons delivered ice in the summer and coal in the winter well into the 1930s.

In winter the sleigh took the children to school and to town.

The two-horse working sleigh carried farmers as well as a box that could be used to carry fodder for the animals.

Life on the farm changed with the arrival of the automobile. Without good roads, the early automobiles and trucks often broke down. With improved roads and sturdier cars, auto sales skyrocketed. An open car on a winter day was still an adventure.

In 1908, Henry Ford introduced the Model T, a tough, simple, cheap car, which was hard to damage and easy to repair. Dairy farmers often converted a sedan into a makeshift pickup to carry the milk cans to town. A blast from the bulb horn cleared the way in the farm yard.

This young man is proudly showing off his Model T (probably the first car owned by the family) to his wife in her long everyday dress.

All dressed up in Sunday finery, a young man had the top up for shade from the sun on his outing. The tool box on the running board was a reminder that breakdowns or flat tires were still an expected part of every trip.

The closed car made driving more comfortable, especially during the winter.

The stylish elegance of this four-passenger car was a marked improvement on previous models. The addition of a spare tire eliminated the need to repair tires on the road, and the lack of a tool box on the running board indicated greater reliability. Life on the farm was becoming closer to that of city dwellers.

The Ford Model A was a major improvement over earlier models. Farmers had their own gas pumps for convenience and savings. Gasoline delivered in bulk to a farm for tractors was cheaper and exempt from taxes.

In 1927, this model had many added features; solid hub wheels instead of spokes, a substantial bumper, and electric head lights made it a dependable form of transportation.

Automobiles were used for fun as well as work. This family is all dressed up for church or for visiting friends or relatives, common Sunday practices.

This Model T was driven to a park for a picnic in 1922. The presence of automobiles in parks and recreation areas spawned a rapid growth as town people wanted to experience the great outdoors.

A snappy Ford Model A coupe suited this well-dressed couple, Mildred and Bill Barth of Prairie View Road in rural Walworth, shown here *c.* 1930. They met while dancing at the Dutch Mill ballroom, near Lake Delavan.

The automobile also offered an alternative to train travel and allowed one to come and go without reference to the train schedules. Travel to Lake Geneva from Chicago took only a few hours on the new federal highways, U.S. 12 and U.S. 14. Bill Barth and his sister took a leisurely ride to California in the late 1920s in his Ford Model A coupe, camping along the way.

One of the first two-car families in Walworth County chose the dependable Ford two-door and a four-door.

Beginning in 1899, an electric trolley shuttled people from Harvard, Illinois, south of Walworth County, to the village of Walworth, and, later, to Fontana on Geneva Lake. By 1927, the service was terminated because of competition from the automobile, and the last tracks were removed before 1950.

What young lady could refuse a drive through the country with this nattily dressed young man in his open Model T?

Cars like this Ford of the early 1930s were sleek and dependable. Frequent trips to Chicago were made easy by the automobile and so spending a summer on Lake Geneva became possible for a greater number of people.

By 1939, Ford built pickup trucks that often replaced the horse-drawn wagons. The pickup saved a great deal of tedious work spent caring for the horses.

Eight

CHANGING STYLES

Both the workday clothes and the Sunday suit of a farmer in 1870 were very different from those of his city cousins. By 1930, the bib overalls still remained in the barns; otherwise, the farmer and his wife began to look very much like the city folk. Hats and beards were very much in vogue for pioneers at the 1897 Walworth County Old Settlers Day.

Mayor Francis of Delavan and his wife posed in the 1870s.

In 1913, this couple looks quite unhappy as they pose in front of their home, which has a fieldstone foundation.

These four generations spanned the period from 1841 to 1920.

Two prominent Elkhorn families were joined when Elizabeth "Lizzie" Weaver married George Moyse at the family home, Maple Lawn Farm, in LaGrange Township on June 6, 1900. George Moyse had the center-part hair style and mustache popular at the time.

This lovely bride wore a two-piece cream silk wedding gown.

Men's fashions did not change as much as women's. The high-starched collar with a different colored vest was fashionable in 1900.

Paul Barth, a first generation immigrant from Germany at age nine, wore a warm matching three-piece suit in 1885.

In the early 1900s, this suit, shirt, and tie were much like those worn in the late 20th century.

Young men's wear changed drastically in the 1940s, when civilian attire was exchanged for military uniforms.

Some women dressed alike, as part of their bond of friendship.

Secrets made life mysterious for these girls, pictured wearing lisle stockings made of shiny strong cotton thread.

These two women share the same long hair style, piled on the top of the head.

Two friends mug for the camera in their high-buttoned shoes in 1921.

Drafty homes meant warm clothing for babies.

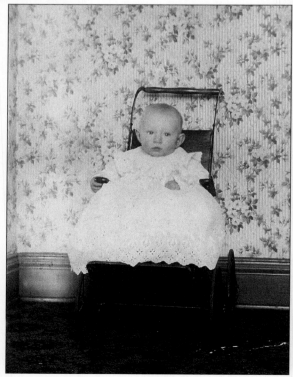

This baby boy looks comfortable in his long eyelet trim dress in a large-wheeled stroller, which moved more easily outdoors over the grass.

This baby, photographed in 1896, wore a long woolen dress for warmth.

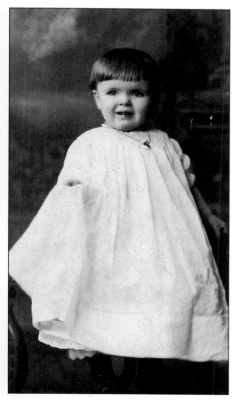

Even children wore high-buttoned shoes.

With the advent of central heating, toddlers' dresses started to shorten in the late 1920s and the 1930s. Shiny leather patent Mary-Jane's and short socks complete this costume.

This little boy posed happily in a very ornate chair.

Long stockings were still used with the Mary-Jane's.

Three siblings, just learning to smile, pose in their warm, long stockings.

Identical smiles identify this brother and sister in their long stockings and high-button shoes, using a piano bench for a prop.

Two smartly dressed brothers, Harvey and Charles, pose for the camera c. 1895.

A girl and her brother (in the chair) pose in a studio *c*. 1900. Boys often wore dresses until they were six years old.

In 1932, this smartly dressed girl, with matching fur trim and hat, wears four-buckle overshoes to ensure warm feet.

The security of being with mother made little grown-ups of this brother and sister, pictured in their high-button shoes and long black stockings.

This young lad and his puppy find comfort in each other through the difficult ordeal of posing for a picture.

This little girl has graduated to socks rolled below the knee.

Genevieve Craney poses for her tenth birthday in 1921, pretty in ruffles and long curls.

Working clothes were needed to chop this pile of wood.

In the early 1930s, the Model A Ford was a backdrop for these siblings, dressed and ready for play.

Planks served as a sidewalk for this farm lady to carry her basket to the house.

Well-patched bib overalls and an old straw hat were comfortable for this farmer in 1913. New overalls were stiff from the sizing in the denim. A few washes removed the sizing, making the overalls soft and comfortable to wear.

Ready for an outing, this family paused in their fine clothing in 1913.

A well-dressed family promoted the hat industry.

A family rests after a vigorous game of croquet.

The horse rests while the family enjoys a picnic on the grass.

A family reunion, with all the men and boys wearing hats and the ladies in long dresses, was an opportunity to show off and catch up on family affairs.

Several decades later, a family reunion shows a change in style with an air of informality, although the ladies dresses remained long. Straw hats replaced the caps and hats.

The changing fashions between 1870 and 1950 are a clear indication that America was becoming one vast middle class with very few rich and relatively few poor at each end of the scale. In 1912, this modest lady even gardened in her long-sleeve, floor-length dress.

Huge puffed "leg-o-mutton" sleeves were popular during the "Gay Nineties."

The long hair styles were abandoned in favor of fashionable bobs in the 1920s. Elsie Barth, who never cut her hair in deference to her father, wore her long hair in a bun.

Hair was puffed out with a pompadour, built up over pads called "rats," during the first decade of the 1900s.

It seemed that every family had dress-up clothes in the latest fashions, even before World War I, and having a portrait dressed in those clothes was a desirable necessity. Elegance describes this dress of ribbed satin.

In 1900, the "S-line" silhouette had a low-pointed bodice and a corset which pushed the bosom forward and the hips back, making the top of the lady almost a foot ahead of the rest of her.

A casual dress emphasized the sailor look in 1913.

Mannish suits were in style in 1913.

The bigger the hat, the more fashionable it was in 1910. Elsie Barth of Walworth was the epitome of elegance, wearing a fur scarf, muff, and large hat secured by long hat pins.

When skirts reached 6 inches off the floor, the gossips raised their eyebrows.

In the 1920s, hemlines were shorter and cloche hats fitted closely to the woman's head.

A lady poses in her shapeless, but easy-to-wear, coat in front of a Model T in 1923.

Nine

EDUCATION AND CHANGES IN SOCIETY

Village schools that drew students from their surrounding areas were large. In 1882, the student body lined up in front of the East Troy School. The long skirts provided warmth in the drafty classrooms.

In the 19th century, school hours were dictated by the needs of the farm. Short hours allowed the students to help milk the cows before and after school, and long summer vacations were needed so that families could work in the fields. The boys and girls of Richmond Center celebrated a sports victory in 1931. All of the boys still wore bib overalls.

Only a few years later, the bib overalls had disappeared, perhaps because this was a dress-up day for the annual photograph. The Blooming Prairie Schoolhouse has been moved to the Walworth County Fair Grounds and remains a memorial to the one-room country schoolhouse. Many small schoolhouses were necessary because the children had to walk to school from widely separated farms.

In 1933, the village school in Walworth had the advantage of a brick building. The dress code had changed to neckties and large hair ribbons.

In 1940, the rural Mickle School in Linn Township, on Swamp Angel Road, still reflected an earlier time, with boys in overalls and high top boots. There were only 17 students in the one-room school.

The modern and durable village of Walworth's red-brick school, built in 1892 for grades one through twelve, still stands as part of the elementary system.

To accommodate the baby boom after World War II, a completely new and separate high school was built, called Big Foot High School after Chief Big Foot, whose Potawatomi tribe was moved to a Kansas reservation in 1836.

Horticultural Hall in Lake Geneva was built in 1912 as a center of social activities such as flower and antique shows. The building was designed by Robert B. Spencer Jr.

When installed, the 40-inch Yerkes telescope was the largest of its type in the world. An advanced educational tool, the telescope was installed on the shores of Lake Geneva at Williams Bay by the University of Chicago to take advantage of the clear sky, far from the polluted air of Chicago. The revolving dome is 90 feet in diameter. Many advanced scholars still do research at the observatory.

Before 1750, there had been little change in the way of life since biblical times. One of Jesus' disciples would have been familiar with most aspects of life in 1700: sailing ships, horse-drawn wagons, paintings, handwritten letters, scythes, and life centered in small agricultural villages with few cities.

Beginning in the mid-18th century, the Industrial Revolution changed almost all everyday implements: steamships, experimental steam cars, printed illustrations, printed books, and early horse-drawn agricultural implements. The factory town replaced the village, and the number of cities increased dramatically.

A second revolution—a technological revolution—from 1880 to 1950 changed the way Americans and Europeans lived to an extent beyond comparison to any other period in history. By 1950, major transformations had occurred: gasoline and diesel engines replaced steam; radio, motion pictures, and television almost replaced the printed word; and the automobile relegated the horse to a recreational role. In 1930, this little girl had a bright new future ahead of her.